BEAUTIFUL CHAOS

OTHER BOOKS BY ROBERT M. DRAKE

SPACESHIP (2012)

SCIENCE (2013)

BLACK BUTTERFLY (2015)

A BRILLIANT MADNESS (2015)

BEAUTIFUL AND DAMNED (2016)

beautiful CHAOS

ROBERT M. DRAKE

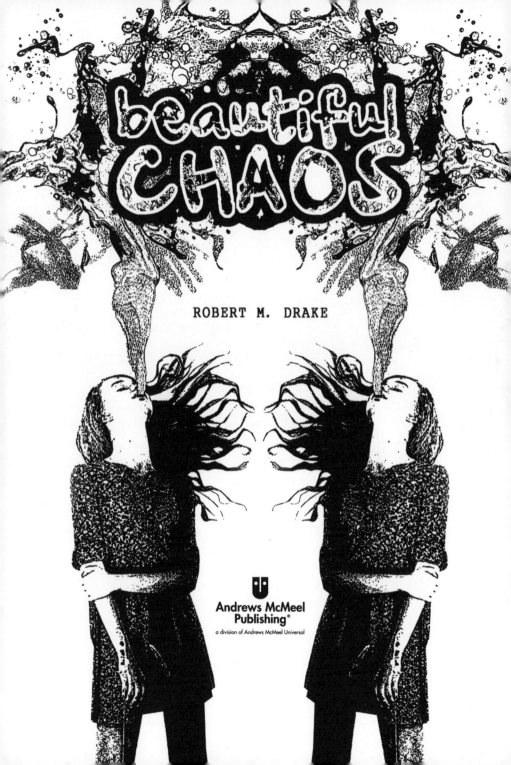

Andrews McMeel
Publishing®

a division of Andrews McMeel Universal

Andrews McMeel Publishing
a division of Andrews McMeel Universal
1130 Walnut Street, Kansas City, Missouri 64106

www.andrewsmcmeel.com

16 17 18 19 20 RR2 10 9 8 7 6 5 4 3 2 1

ISBN: 978-1-4494-8478-1

Library of Congress Control Number: 2016946132

Book design: Robert M. Drake

First Edition 2013

Dedicated to Sevyn.

Little girl do not grow up too fast,
and if you can, do not grow up at all.

Grown-ups are sour and dull,
they lack so much, too much.

Do not grow up too fast, try not to at all.
The older you get the harder it will be.

You will learn how there is not much to look forward to.
Things are so much better when you are young.

So little girl, try not to grow, avoid it.
Watch cartoons and read books.
Stay up late and make art.
Keep pushing yourself and never stop believing.

The moment you stop is the moment you lose it all.

Childhood is a spark, once you lose it, you will
never get it back, but if you protect it,
it will grow with you and the more you have it,
the more inspired you will be.

The world is much more
beautiful when it is seen through
the eyes of a child.

So please, do not grow too fast,
and if you can, not at all.

The world is filled

with broken people

with broken lives

searching for broken love.

And that is why being

alone has never

felt so good.

I can't see myself

with the crowd.

I never have.

People need people.

People need love.

They need to love themselves

the way they love

what they are sold.

CONTENTS

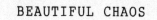

BEAUTIFUL CHAOS

This is

a manifestation

of the chaos

we harbor inside.

And it is all

so beautiful.

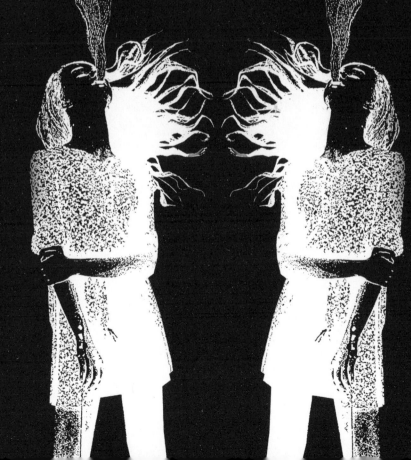

Forever.

Forever Is Forever

Forever
does not seem
too far away.

Sometimes it is
after we lose someone
when we learn
to love.

Where hope,
and dreams greet,
and everything is perfect
the way
it was meant to be.

So hear me,
soon enough
we will meet again
old friend.

I will carry your soul
in my heart.

The same heart you
helped me build.

Don't worry.

Beating The Brain

Do not
worry little one.
I am here.
I am always beside you.
I cannot leave.
I don't know how to.

People will tell you
they will never leave you.

That is bullshit.
The ones who tell you that,
are the first to make you feel alone.

"I will never leave you."
"I will always love you."

People who love you
do not need to constantly remind you.

They are the ones
who cannot walk away.

They are the ones
who are still here.

Keep looking.

Look Deeper

Look deeper through
the telescope
and
do not be afraid when the stars
collide toward the darkness,
because sometimes,
the most beautiful things
begin in chaos.

Crash and burn.
Let it all fuse into one.

Let it all collide
the way two people exchange
eyes
when they meet for the
very first time.

Little Note:1

Do not worry,
little heart.

They are only
feelings...

So care a little less.
The ride will be
much more
than what it
seems.

Little Note:2

I never understood us,
for how can something
so special
cause so much
pain after all...

Maybe we are too human
and disaster trails
behind us.

All is lost here.

All Is Lost Here

O sweet child,
but we are all
lost here.
So close those
tired eyes
and
follow where your
heart leads.

Follow the ruins.
Follow the sorrow.
Follow the darkness.

We are all living
the same story.

We are all a little
lost and mad.

Madly in love with the way
we lose ourselves,
and find the courage to believe,
in all the things that help us
find our way.

Just a little push.

Just A Little Push

All
she needed
was
a little push,
to feather
into the arms
of the
one
she loved.

Between the sea and the sky.

The Sea And The Sky

It is written between the sea
and the sky, within the horizon rests
that word. The word neither science
nor religion can make sense of.
The word to end and start all wars.
The word we use to express something
greater than ourselves.

The word we die for.
We live for and look for when it
cannot be seen.

It is written.
Written over the stars so we can
wish for it.
So when we look closer,
just a little closer,
we will discover...

All that we are
and
all that we will ever be
is love.

Devour.

Devour

Devour me
with the rawness,
the raw shred of me.
Break me down, grab me,
destroy me
and never fade gently
into the dark.

Swallow me.
Twist me.
Crush me.
For I am yours...

Crave me
and look for me in the
heat of the storm.

And when it is over...
I will still
rip you apart
for all that you are.

I am consumed.

Little Note:3

A touch
of Madness
will
always
be stored
in the
crater
of love.

Little Note:4

Every
magic moment
will bring
you closer to your
dreams.

Fall in love.

Falling Free

I want us to fall
in love like drops of rain,
not these small passing showers.
I need wind.
I need lightning.
I need trees blown off their roots.

I want us to fall
into each other.
Into the hollowness of
our souls.

We are all a little empty inside.
All I want is you.

You to fill me
even if it is only
for a little
while.

Call my own.

Call My Own

It is not that I
want the simple.
It is more like that is all
I know.

The simple is all we know.
The easy way out and the easy
way in.

I look up at the sky
and it is all full
of lights,
and my arms are too short
to reach one
to call my own.

Life is better looking down.
Everything up is impossible.

Everything up I have to work
for
to call my own.

Fall apart.

Apart

Things fall apart.
Things speed up and then
they slow down.

We were evolving into something,
something greater, perhaps,
too much for our own good.

Things come together.
Things slow down and then
they speed up again.

We must all move on
and I
understand that.

I think we all do,
but still,
I will leave a little bit
of love
somewhere inside me
just in case
if you ever decide to return
home.

Let us go.

Let Us Go

Come away with me.
Let us go somewhere.

You and me.
The two of us...

Let us find the darkness
and let us find
the light.

I want us to forget our worries
and do all the things we want
today.

We should all do the things
today, that will help us build
a better tomorrow.

Tomorrow is always waiting
for more.

Little Note:5

Burn away
and burn every burning
sorrow
that burns
you like a burning
star,
and awaken all that
you would burn for
to burn every burning
scar.

Little Note:6

Danger
will always
chase her
and she will
always
greet it
with a smile.

Explore.

Explore

Always explore the world.
See it with new eyes.
I know it is easier said than done.

But
imagine what it is like to feel
the same way you did last year...
to feel the same way over something
new and different.

Imagine this.
Imagine that.

Dream of new places.
Places you could not even begin to imagine.

Those places are out there.
Those places are waiting.
Waiting for people like us to fill them,
and for people like us
to make sense of
why these places exist
to begin with.

Let us go.
Let us not be afraid.

Every night.

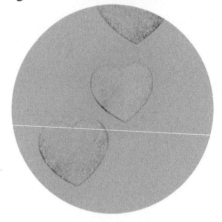

Every Night

Every night
I go back to the strands
of your memory
and some nights I would
surrender and let go.

Letting go...
that is a beautiful thing.

Letting go...
it is something we all should do.

Because one night is not
enough.
It is never enough—it starts
a fire, out of control.

I had to learn to let go,
I always found myself
wanting more.

Every night I wanted to burn.
Every night I could not
let go.

Not like you.

God In You

Dear God,

I am not like you.
I am weak, my bones are brittle,
my heart is filled with darkness
and at times my demons crawl
out from the walls you built.

I am just an extension of you,
of all that you are...
but what would it be like
to become a wave in an ocean of
you.

I am lost in your shine
and I drown in your touch.

Dear God,

So maybe I have ignored you
lately,
but this is me reminding you
that I, too, suffer
and I, too, seek
the beauty in humanity.

So hear me, you are not alone.

Rid me.

Rid Me To Nothing

Rid me of all that has
ever ruined me,
and this darkness that consumes
the life in me.

Rid me of brokenness
and even wholeness.

Rid me of all the things that fill you empty.

Rid me in pieces, rid me to nothing,
but leave just enough of me to grow.

Rid me to rid me in you,
and not a second less...
fill me with all that makes you
expand in such a small room.

Rid me my love,

rid me of all, till I am nothing.
Till I am something, you need.

I want to spill over you and leave no
trace behind.
No trace to spoil of you to rid me
inside.

Little Note:7

Imagine
what we would
all
accomplish
together,
if we left
our egos
at the door.

Little Note:8

So laugh a little more,
care a little more,
and love a little more,
for all we will
ever be
is what we become.

And in the end,

we will become
all the things
we leave behind.

Cycle.

Seconds And Hours

I will be
whatever you want me to be.
Does that sound awful?

I will be your spring,
if you will be my summer.

I will be your fall,
if you will be my winter.

We will cycle
and cycle
until forever breaks the seconds
and the seconds break the hours.

Every moment we spend
is every moment we have been
looking for,
for so long.

Too human.

Human Suffering

Maybe all of this.
All of this hurt
and all of this pain
and suffering is something
only humans can endure.

This all follows us
like a bad habit, impossible to let go.
The pain is all we know.
At most, the pain is what we stay
attracted to.

It is the only thing that defines me
and defines all of us as humans.

It is the only way we know how to
connect with each other.

This pain.
This hurt.
This suffering.

It is all too human,
and as humans
it is all too beautiful to ignore
after all.

Words.

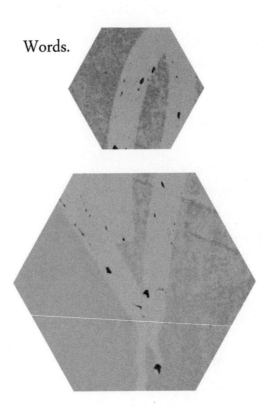

Inspiring

This woman I met
a long time ago,
she said I had a way with words
and I said she had a way
with laughter.

It spoke to me
the way imagination speaks to a child.

I told her without her
there would not be any of me
or any of my words.

She never understood this,
she was my words
and I was her laughter.

And in the end, there were no words
and there was no laughter.

Just a blank space,
a blank face
that none of us would even
dare to understand.

Make you beautiful.

Mirrors

Some people feel ugly.
It is not because they do not
attract other people
or because they are not adored.

It is because they do not see
themselves.
They do not see their light.

Their reflection.

Sometimes,
you have to shatter
the mirror in you,
to see all the pieces
that make the sun in you,
flare
in the middle of the crowd.

Little Note:9

He returned to her
and his lips awakened every atom
in her body.

His love exhausted her stars,
she could not help it.

She stumbled,
and lost her balance because of him.

She wrapped herself in his
moonlight,
and
forever she stayed...

And she seasoned his love.

Little Note:10

Maybe her story does not
have an ending.

Maybe God will remember her
and wheel her
through the air,
so we can all breathe
her in...

and exhale her
brilliance
through the wind.

Broke.

Broke Myself

I broke myself
beautiful
when I left you;
it was me
saving
me
from myself.

And it was me
breaking me
from everything else.

Funny way.

Repeating Itself

You said your heart
had been broken
and if I believed enough
we would be forever.

I guess history has a funny
way of repeating itself.

And it is a shame how
everything
meaningful must end...

Especially when
everything I had,
everything inside me,
was everything I gave you
to make your own.

Conquer the demons.

Demons

Everyone has
their own battle.

That is the obvious.

We all tend to dive into
ourselves from time
to time.

But if there is
something to be learned,
something to be felt
or something to be done

it is this:

To conquer the demons in you
before letting
the demons in others
conquer you.

There is no other way
to survive or to die,
that is, to go on
by the hand of your own
darkness.

The world.

Listen Well

Be authentic
to yourself and to those
around you.

Open your mind.
Open your heart.
Your eyes,
your mouth, and your hands.

You will find there is more.
There always will be...
This life is filled with greed,
sin and sadness.

Stay true to the bone of your skull,
listen well my sweet little love.
If you must cheat,
cheat yourself out of the
lies this world created.

For only the real survive.
Only the real can build the
foundation.

Fuck the lies and everything else.

Little Note:11

We all can
learn how to breathe
submerged;

we just have to
find
that one person
worth
drowning for.

Little Note:12

Let your love
flow where the
beautiful things are
and
something beautiful
will always
come your way.

Drizzle.

Falling Apart

I am slowly
falling apart, scorching away.
My ashes drizzle
and I have destroyed myself
to wind over your shore,

to remind you how
someone out there
is still burning for you.

Burning for the
blooming flower in your
soul.

And it is such
a beautiful way to
fall apart.

To lose myself above
the ocean.

Above the skin
without knowing what
dwells beneath it all.

About myself.

Finding It

And loving you
was a pattern of self-discovery
because someway, somehow,
I always ended up
learning something new
and something real about myself.

So thanks baby,
thank you for the fucking
hurting
and the beating
and the tragic love story
and the way you handled it,
the way you let go.

It helped me learn one thing.

How some people really do need
other people.
How they need someone to tear them apart,
until there is nothing
left to hold.

And I am holding on to whatever it is
that I have left.

To all the things you left behind.

A million pieces.

A Million Pieces

People break
other people.
This I know.
That is not a secret
or
some kind of rare thing
to live through.

It is full of sadness
and sorrow
and all things that are black
and terrible.

But there you are,
a strong
gentle woman
and
I would break into
a million pieces,
if only,
it meant a million pieces
of me to call your
own.

Being burned.

An Idea

She sold the idea well.
The words "I love you"
flowed from her mouth.

I was married to this idea.
It felt like being burned
alive and I took the pain.
It was all I could do,
just take it like it was all I was born
to do.

Over and over...without wake.

I was hers and she was mine.

Over and over...coming and going.

People have a strange way of finding
their way.

People are strange and my way will
always lead back to her.

No matter how far I go.
I will find her, I was sold on this
idea since the beginning of
it all.

Little Note:13

We are like
astronauts:

Dreaming on the moon.
Telescoping the stars.
Exploring the skies,
and searching for the
moments
that take our
breath away.

Little Note:14

Be you.

Be original.

Be all the things
they say you
cannot be.

Rebellion is the key.

Break the rules,
and you will find
something they
have never seen before.

Charge in me.

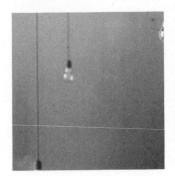

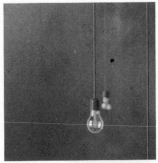

Burning Lovers

There is a charge in me.
It burns for you.
It burns from my eyes,
to my heart and to my skin.

I want to collect all the pieces.
All the things that bring
out the goodness in you and in
all people.

I want to peel away all the hurting
out of you.

Do not be afraid
when I give you all my years,
my hours and my seconds.

Every moment I spend
finding you,
is every moment I spend
finding myself as well.

My love is your love, my love,
and it is the only reason
worth burning all the things
we love.

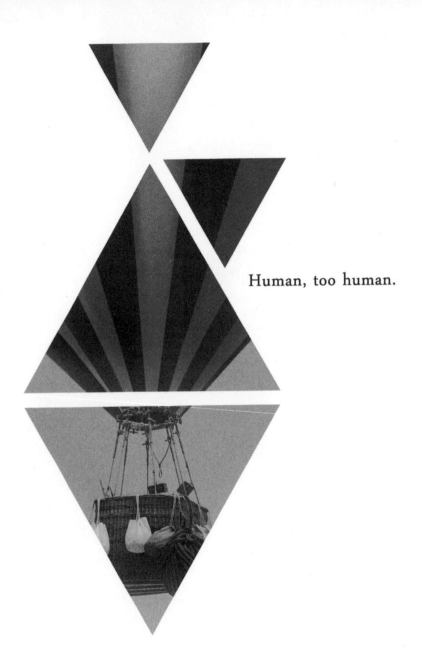

Human, too human.

I Saw Her

She went on.
She became human.
I saw her for all her flaws.
For all the pain she had
buried in her eyes.

Those eyes...

That fire.
That horror.
That terrible,
terrible light.

Those eyes...
have seen too much.
Too much humanity.
Too much of all the things
she wants to forget.

I saw her for her flaws,
but in the end,
I, too, saw her for all
the goodness that clung to her
like the life she wanted.

I saw her for who she was.

A strong woman.

Violently missing you.

I Will Miss You

I do miss you.
It is simple.
There is no other way to put it.

I miss you, all of you, for all that you are.
It kills me how you linger
so close.
It kills my day
and my night.

I will never be at ease
while watching the sunset,
knowing how our story
will never end with the same words.

All sunsets have their own
story,
it is that ours
will always fall shy,
and it will always fall
incomplete.

I will miss you.

Madness.

Troubles

I am in trouble.
I have been trying to make
sense of myself.

I have been trying to make
sense of the world.

I think every hour,
every second
and every moment.

I am in trouble.

I knew this kind of sadness
was in me,
but
I had no clue how to surface it.

I am in trouble.

I am in the grave.

I am in love with a woman,

and she has no clue how I feel.

Little Note:15

Look at the system.

Low-paying jobs.
GMOs in foods.
High taxes.
High rent.
High gas prices.
Unlawful arrest.

The list can go on.

Drowning. Drowning. Drowning.

And not enough
opportunity to help us
rise beyond
the shallow stream.

Little Note:16

The universe
is watching you.

So be a nice human.

Magic moments.

Why I Write

She wants to love, she says.
She tells me she wants to remember
what it is like to feel appreciated.
To feel the sudden rush
of someone worth it, someone to
keep her up at night.

The mind is as wild as the heart.

Too many fucked up relationships
will do that to you.
So I get it, believe me I really do.

This woman told me her story,
and she broke it down to the details.

By the end of the night, I
saw a different kind of person
sitting before me.
When people are open you see them
for who they are,

and for once I understood her,
I understood people.

All we really want is someone to listen to
our sorrows.

Burn away.

Women

"Would you stay?"

I thought about it for a second.
Not because I couldn't stay,
but because I couldn't make sense of
it.

Women are sweet little things.
They will terrorize a man with
just a few words.

"Would you stay?" she said, as she
blocked the door.

I looked dead into her eyes.
I wanted to go but I couldn't.

It wasn't that easy.
Women aren't that easy.
This love thing isn't that easy.

She just took everything from me.

"Would you just stay? I'm sorry," she said.

She took it all and I walked back
into her room.

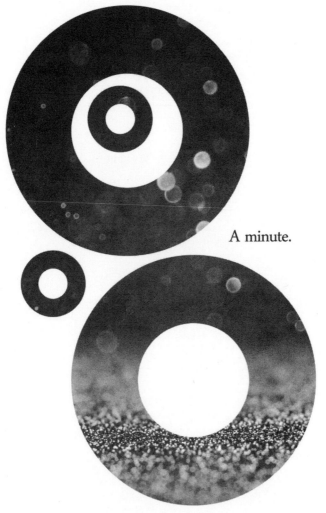

A minute.

In The Right Place

All she needed
was a minute
to fall in love
with all the stars.

With all the night
and all the day.

With the way the world
took her breath,
and with the way
her life took a different
turn.

Things change...

and after that night
it all just changed.

She believed
and
that is all she needed.

That night she inspired me.
That night I, too,
had changed.

Sometimes.

Not Myself

Sometimes,
I feel like I don't know
myself
like I'm lost inside myself.

And I can't even live within myself,
and I can't trust myself
when I'm by myself.

Too many broken pieces
scattered of myself,
too empty and maybe I'm not myself.

I think I need you to save
me from myself

because without you
I'm just not myself.

Little Note:17

There is a way in everything.

If you only believe.

Believing makes the impossible,
possible and everything else

real.

Little Note:18

You are marvelous.
You are brilliant.
You are more than what
I expect you to be.

Be more.
Be less.
Be something they
cannot put on their fingers.

Be something
out of this world.

Danger.

What We Are Meant To Do

People will do whatever they
are meant to do.

No matter what is going on.
If the world is ending.
If the world is burning.
If the world has gone mad.

People will do whatever they
are meant to do.

No matter what it is.
No matter where they are.
No matter what horrors are manifested.

People will do whatever they
are meant to do.

People are born to live.
People are born to die.

People will do whatever they
are meant to do.

So worry less...
You will soon get there.

Please understand.

Things We Don't Need

Please understand that without you
I cannot finish the day.
I cannot rest buried only in light.

I, too, need darkness to close my eyes
and dream.

I, too, need to feel the coldness
of the night and I, too, need your
shade to hang over my tired eyes.

I cannot find the words to describe
why I need you.

I need you, and
that alone is enough to define it all.

I need you.

I need your soul, your art, your madness,
I need it all.

I now understand why people fall in love.

Always.

Through The Fire

You will always
be beautiful,
before and after today.

When our days have seen age.
Two tired souls.
Two tired hearts.

We have been through it all,
through the fire,
and still,
what once was will always remain.

You will always be inside me.

Never forget that.

Never forget how much I lived
for you, how much I exhausted my hours
to watch you grow.

Never forget how much I loved,
and above all,
never forget me for how
my bones made love to yours
every time I saw you walk away.

Imagine.

Don't Come Late

The things I am afraid of.

I can't listen to myself
anymore, there must be something
inside my soul.

Something I can't make sense of,
but I know it is there.

Into the night.
Into the day.
All these years and I still can't
figure it out.

I still can't understand
all of this love inside me.

I still don't know what I
can do with it.

What it was meant for.

Maybe one day it will all make sense.

Just don't come too late.

Little Note:19

Today is a good
fucking day.

So grab a drink and enjoy
yourself.

The next day might not
be what it is
you expect.

Live in the moment.

All else means nothing.

Little Note:20

If there is nothing
good here,
then why dwell on it so much?

The world needs you,
all of you.

So stop focusing on the
little things that
do not matter.

Bigger things are ahead,
make the move,

you deserve this.

We both saw ourselves.

Compare

She said she loved
the ocean,
and I said I loved
the stars,
and for the first time
we agreed on
something.

We both saw ourselves
loving the things we
dreamed of,
and ignored everything
that made us beautiful.

And because of this...

We were never born
into what they wanted
us to believe.

Behind.

The People Are Lost

No one ever thinks
they are mad.
The mad don't say they are,
they don't know it.

I have been called mad.
I don't see it.

I sit down and look at the people.
Alone and thinking.

They all look mad,
walking somewhere as if they are late.
Walking, looking at their phones.
Walking, looking at the floor, the sky.
Walking, looking into their souls.

These people have lost it.
These people keep walking.

They are lost and they are all
searching for more.

The lost don't ever know they are lost
they just keep going
and they will go until they
can't go anymore.

Fools rush in.

Fools Rush

Let us go to a place

where no one knows
us,
and find our smiles.

Let us go to a place

where we can wander,
and find our laughter.

Let us go to a place

where we can find ourselves,
and find innocence again.

Let us go to a place

where we can fall
and find a love to catch us,
and take us
to a place where
only fools rush in.

Footprints.

Walk Slowly

Maybe all the broken
dreams and empty
promises the world offered
are just reflections
of what is within us.

Maybe one day
we will learn to accept
ourselves
for all the faults
sleeping
beneath the footprints
we leave behind.

Little Note:21

Take the beating.

The world is hard,
so take it
until you become the pain
that caused you
the hurting.

That is what real
power is all about.

Little Note:22

Breathe the love.
Become the love.

That is where
the legends die.

That is where
you will live forever.

Myself without you.

It's Late

It was late
but I wanted her to
come away with me.
I wanted her
to run with me in the dark.

The same way we chase
the things we know
are no good for us.

It was late
I wanted her to come.
I promised all types
of things I knew I couldn't
keep.

And like us all
we fall into people
regardless if good or bad,
we fall inside others
because that is,
after all,
the only thing we know
how to do.

Belong.

Oceans Apart

We all could be great,
and leave our dreams
on the shore,
drift away and still believe
that the best is yet to come.

And even after everything,
even after the tide
brings us back to where
we end.

I would still feel
empty knowing we drifted
apart,
and how you are only
an ocean away from being
where you belong.

I will find you.
I will never let you go.

Oceans are not easy to forget
or to remember,
but oceans are meant to be explored.

I will find you,
and I am holding my breath until
I do.

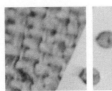

Felt lost.

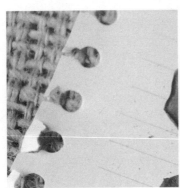

Her Blooming Heart

She always felt lost
and it was beautiful not
knowing how she would
find herself.

I watched her,
I watched her bloom
into this sweet flower.

She didn't know where she
was meant to go,
but I knew...

I knew because women like her
were born to start fires.

Born to change men.
Born to end men.

I knew she was something else.
Something great like a light
exploding in the back of our eyes.

I believed,
and it was only a matter of time,
till
all of her made sense.

Returned.

Tragic Lovers

I returned to this woman.
I knew she was no joke.

This woman would exhaust me.
My mind.
My thoughts.
My heart.

Any woman could destroy a man,
but when she is gone,
he regains whatever is left
and soon enough he is himself again.

This woman was no walk in the park.
She took everything from me,
all the things that mattered
and every time I saw her,
I gave in to her.

There is no other way to explain
this madness.
This coming and this going.

I wanted her
and when I had her
I would always lose a piece
of myself.

Little Note:23

Thank God every day,
and if you do not
believe in God,

then thank life for
all the blessings it
has granted you.

Little Note:24

Mistakes are gifts.

Every day you make
mistakes.

How you take it
is how you will be rewarded

in the end.

The wind.

Stories Go To The Sky

I don't want to end.
I don't want to be forgotten.
I don't know how to be, and I still don't
know how to be a memory.

Remember me.
Remember why you should remember me.

Remember what it is like
to be floating inside
someone.
To be exhaled back into the wind.

I want you to remember
how I was inside of you,
and how terrible it was when you
let me go.

Now I am everywhere,
in the air, in the sky and in the clouds.

Look around you, I am around you,
and the love you let go
belongs to a world,
a burning world which consumes your burning soul.

You can't forget that feeling.
You can't forget me.

Wild things.

The Things We Are

We are beautiful things.
We are wild things.

Searching for the brilliance
within us.

We are all these things.
Things we can't begin to imagine.
Things with spaces inside.
We are looking for something,
anything,
to show us a direction,
a manifestation,
a clue...

To why we have so much inside
us,
and so little time
to make sense of all
the things that make us
who we are.

Feels like the sunset.

Missing You Feels...

Missing you
feels like the sunset
and not a night
goes by
where I walk toward
the shore,
wishing you would
shipwreck
and just stay home.

Missing you
feels like the tired moon.
Alone at night
and waiting for something
different to happen,
like you,
coming back to me,
and
not knowing where
or how to go

anywhere else
other than where
you know
you belong.

Little rebel.

She Part 2

She had a little rebel in her.
A little chaos and a little gentleness.
She did not say much,
and sometimes she would doze off.
She would drift away, dream with the stars
and that was okay.

She had a little fight in her,
and every time she built a little
courage, her voice would
echo through the sky.

She was not complete,
but she had enough.
There was a science to her genius,
her madness,
her beauty and there was nothing
she could not accomplish.

She was unstoppable...

And everything she ever wanted
she took with nothing
but a smile.

Little Note:25

The coffin is the truth.

No lies can go beyond there.

Little Note:26

There is almost no time
for anything anymore.

Find the seconds to tell
someone you love them.

They might be gone the
next time you
say their name.

Inside us.

A Flame In The Light

I knew it was not meant to work out.

There was just too much inside us.
Maybe it was love,
or maybe it was something else,

because we had something else.
Something terrible but it was
so goddamn hard to ignore.

A match.
A light.
A fire.
A star.

All burning, together
and all at once.

It felt good when she was around.
I felt different.

And although we knew how it was going
to end, we still tried it.

It was something the body
needed to feel the soul.

Dear you.

Dear You

Every gust of wind
carries your voice.
Every sunrise radiates the warmth
derailing from your smile.
Every ocean reflects the shades
seasoning from your eyes,
and during the night I can see everything
you have ever wanted me to see.

Every star exhales your favorite stories,
wrapped in a fabric of dreams.

Your dreams.

Every mountain, summit top and meadow
reminds me of your scripting skin.
And I know you, too, are broken,
and every living creature that
breathes your voice, feels your smile,
vessels in your eyes,
runs through your skin
and looks up at the sky to understand
your story,
has a little piece of you inside them
to call their own.

One day.

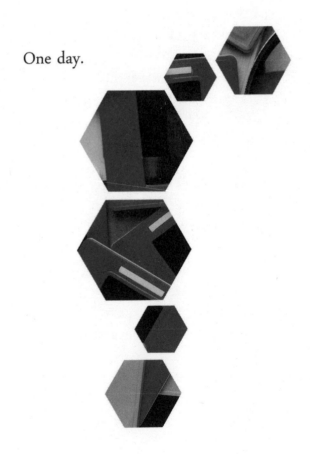

One Day Never Ends

One day someone will inspire you,
and a love will chalk over
your walls.

The sun will love you
and follow you
and you will walk in the sunshine.

It will not kill you.
It will not burn you.

It will push you toward the edge.
And you will inspire people
and continue to be inspired
and you will never destroy these moments.

The moments where you and the light
will meet.

You will never end.

The love inside you will never end.

The glory of the Gods
will glow off you.

Become it.

Becoming Without Me

She became it.
I couldn't believe it.
All this time
ignoring this love.

A love she needed and craved.

Absorbed in and out.
"Don't let it out, dear."
I would say.

There is nothing else to say,
she was different.

The same wild hair.
The same stare.
The same smile and walk.

But this love I had, meant nothing...

After all these years,
I couldn't believe this.

The more she went on to forget
love, the closer she went on to become it.

A love that did not know who I was.

Little Note:27

And just like
everyone else,

I am a few minutes late

from becoming,

from blooming into
something the rain
can relate to.

I am falling for more.
Falling for the love
the world is trying to hide.

Little Note:28

What place is this?

You are lost
and this is nowhere.

Nowhere is closer
to somewhere,
and it is closer
than you think.

Your voice.

There Is Air In You

In your voice,
I can hear a hundred years of music.
A thousand years of the stars colliding.
A million years of everything beyond us.

I have been listening...

Listening to all of you come together,
and now I understand...

I understand why we are vessels
submerged in something great.
Something that becomes one in the shore.

I have always drowned in you.

Forever...till we become a distant memory.

We are more.
We are not scattered.
We are together in one place,
forever...

I will run in you...

The only place where I know
I can breathe.

Learn.

The Growing Tide

I wish I can see you,
not because I miss you,
but because I know I am different now.

When we were together,
I just didn't know
or understand anything about you.

You wanted to be so many things.

Every month you were changing.

You wanted to sing.
You wanted to dance.
You wanted to drink.
You wanted to be so many things.

A different person every hour.

I tried to tame the flame in you.

Maybe being different is just
what made me love you
and maybe it is what makes you
who you are.

Awaken.

There Is A Diamond In You

Stop looking for something
when something
has already found you.

You have been living with
your eyes closed.

Awaken.

It is there.

Take it.

It is yours.

It could all be yours.
Everything.

If only you believe in all
the things that
stir inside of you.

You are marvelous.
You are what you have been
looking for.

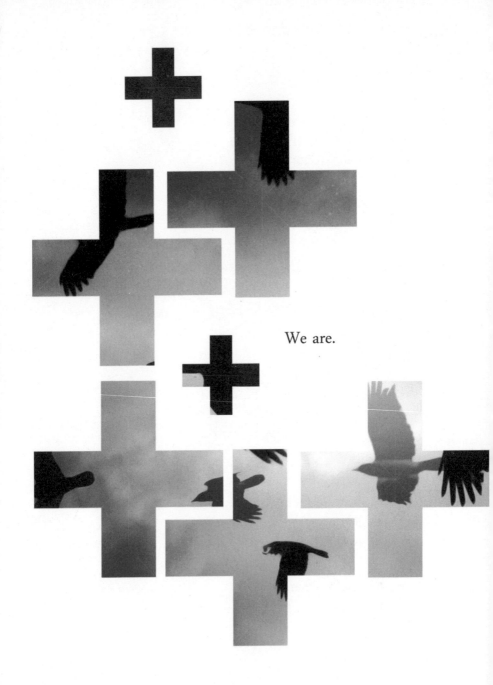

We are.

Science And Chemistry

We are
93 million miles
from the sun.
238 thousand miles
from the moon.
A moment
from finding magic,
and one kiss away
from reaching
our dreams.

Little Note:29

The pain can go on
as long as you let it
go on.

Stop the bullshit.
Cut it out of your life
then let it back in.

That is how you will grow.

Little Note:30

You cannot control everything,
but if there is something
you can control,

it is this:

The education you open
yourself to.

You can learn
and become anything,
as long as you put the work in.

We collide.

Earth, Wind, Fire

We will collide in the air.
We will collide in the water.
We will collide in the moments we ignore.

We will crash,
and we will lose ourselves.

Now listen...

You will be the clouds
and I will be the sky.
You will be the ocean
and I will be the shore.
You will be the trees
and I will be the wind.
You will be the stars
and I will be the moon.
You will be the sunset
and I will be the horizon.

Whatever we are...

You and I will always collide.

Little heart.

Where Does It All Go?

The wind will call our names one day.
It will claim us.
It will not forget us
the way people forget us
if we are no good to them.

People forget people
if they become completely useless to them.

Usefulness is something
we cannot hold on to forever.

People will forget us.
Long after the light in our eyes
leaves our skulls.

The world will go on.
People will go on.
It will all go on.

But the wind...
That is where the breath flows.
That is where we all go in the end.

We are all remembered in the wind.

I will be waiting for you there
and I will not forget your name.

Beautiful things.

Bones And Flowers

There is something
flowing inside of you,
growing, rooting from your bones.

I know you do not know what it is.
Neither do I,
but I know there is something there.

It is fucking beautiful.
It does not leave you alone.
It follows you, trailing
behind you like a comet.

Burning and stretching.
Lighting the night sky, haunting it.

I can see you in the darkness.
I can see it moving.

No matter how far you go.
It is there.

Do not fear the things inside you, my love.

It is beyond the dirt.

Bloom like the flower
you were born to be.

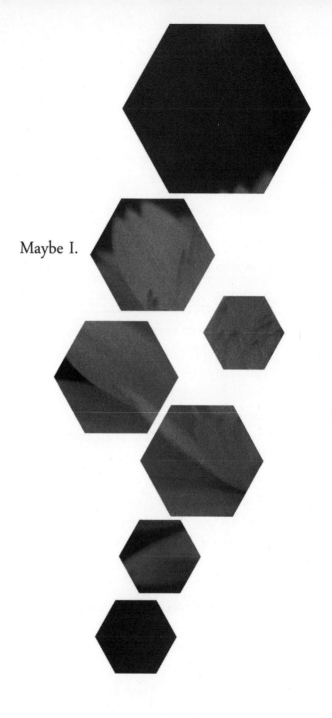

Maybe I.

Too Little Too Much

Peel me down
to the bone,
and you will see,
that I am more than what
people expect me to be.

I am more fire than water.
I am more wind than air.
I am more light than dark.
I am more like you
and less like them.

More soul.
More pain.
More blood.
More human.

This they will never know.
What I am trying to say is:

Maybe I love too much
and maybe I show it too
little.

Little Note:31

It could all
be so beautiful

as long as you

let it consume you.

Little Note:32

Ride the night into
holy happiness.
Ride it until you cannot
any longer or
until, the happiness cannot
hold you.

And you will feel
like the burning sun
the gods left inside of you.

We should all live
for moments like these.

Dreaming on the moon.

I Am Looking Inside Walls

What are you searching for
my love?

You want more don't you?

We all do.
We all want to be loved
and appreciated,
ultimately.

We search the searched for
validation,
and we keep searching through
the same places.

It is endless
and it hurts how much we search
and find nothing.

We become nothing.
Eventually we feel nothing.

And when we find what it is we have been
searching for...

We have nothing left to offer it,
just the empty space we created
ourselves.

You will meet.

Two Pieces Looking For A Home

Goddamnit!

You don't get it, do you?

You walk around
like you're waiting to die.
You breathe in air as if it is not
keeping you alive.

You want to stop
and you want all of it to end
without a fight.

My love, do you not understand?

Somewhere someone
is thinking of you.
Wishing one day
somewhere somehow you
will meet.

Believe in this...
Your sweet flame is out there
and they are waiting for you too.

It is all a matter of time.

It always is.

Too many little.

In The Mirror

She destroyed herself,
too many little thoughts.
She fell apart,
too many little pieces.
She lost herself,
too many little places.
She fell in love,
too many little feelings.
She discovered herself,
too many little stars.
She believed,
too many little moments.

And in the end,

she was home,
too many little things
that reminded her
of herself.

Think you are.

Blindness Is Easy

You are
only as
free
as you
think you are,
and
freedom
will always
be as
real
as you
believe
it to be.

Freedom
is the
illusion.

The illusion
is what is real.

I see what is real,
do you?

I am free,
are you?

Little Note:33

The darkest dark
does not fear
the brightest light.

So why should you
fear your deepest fears?

None of that would matter
with a little courage.

It is in you.
Find it and set it free.

Little Note:34

Everything comes back around,
but there are some things
that keep diminishing as time
goes on.

The hours we are given since birth,
and the love we give to the world.

Both dissolving into the air.

The world makes it hard
to find real love, and time is
running out.

Stop running and the answers will appear.

Maybe that is the real problem.

We began to believe.

Believe In Yourself

I want to teach you
how to dream...
as lovely as that sounds.

I want to teach you how to love.
How to save you
from yourself.

I can see the struggle in you.
In your skull
and in your chest, beating out of you.

You are worth it my dear,
and regardless if you stay
here
or go somewhere else.

I need you to understand
you are worth saving.

It is just no one can save you,
but yourself.

And you will be saved
the moment you begin
to believe.

The stars.

Complicated And Easy

Loving a woman is easy.
I cannot understand
a man when he weeps,
and believes it is impossible.

Women want a few things.
They do not want the spinning universe.

They don't want the youth
of the gods.

Listen well young man.

Do not promise her
the stars if you cannot
see them yourself,
and never tell her you love
her if love does not
mean the world to you.

The answers are that far,
and that close.

They have always been.

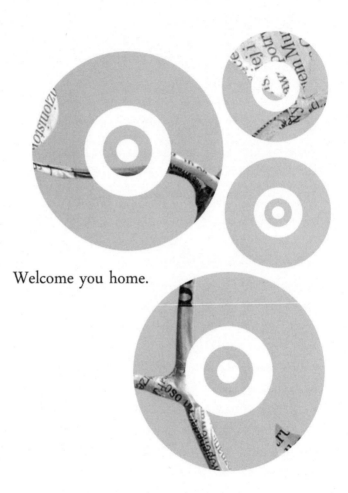

Welcome you home.

In The Eyes

One day
you will make
peace
with your
demons,
and the chaos
in your heart
will
settle flat.

And
maybe
for the first time
in your life...

Life will smile
right back at you
and
welcome
you home.

Those eyes.

Live And Die For You

Those eyes
have seen
so many places,
and that heart
has felt
so many things...

and yet,
you smile at the
darkest feelings
and find
expression
in everything
that is colored
beautiful.

And to me...
there is nothing more
marvelous
than that.

I see you,
and I love you
for who you are.

Little Note:35

To love anything
is a brave thing,
a lovely thing.

So stay brave
and keep on loving.

Kings have built their
kingdoms off this power.

It is the secret they
have kept to themselves
for so long.

Little Note:36

One day they will
come for me,
and when they do
I will be ready.

Beyond the ordinary.

The Stars And The People

We cannot deny
how the world makes us feel.
It pulls us down.
It makes us feel worse
about being ourselves.

Goddamnit, people don't
think that way, look that way, feel that way.

We cannot afford to live so lavishly.
The way millionaires live.
The way movie stars and models live.

Hell, they make everything look so perfect.

I could hardly pay my rent.
I could hardly live at all.

The world makes it too hard to live.

We are not the lights in the sky.
We are the space around the lights.

And we are all trapped,
hoping one day to become more
than that of the black which supports
the stars.

She was.

It Lasted A Moment

This girl
was a lot like the ocean,
a lot like
the wind,
and a lot like the
stars.

She taught me
how to drown
and feel things
above the sky.

If loving you.

Why People Die

Tell me,
what is it all worth?

All this pain.
All this love.

Are these even real?

Some say we all die three times
during our lifetime.

One: When you lose a good friend.
It is always the good ones who die young.

Two: When you let go of bad habits.
It is always the bad ones that kill us
a litte more.

Three: When you meet the love of your
life for the very first time.

And I have been
dying ever since I was born,
but if loving you kills me tonight,
then I will be waiting for death
until you say hello.

Sometimes I do not.

Nights Are Bright

There are days
when I do not feel,
and there are nights
when feeling is just too
damn much for me.

I do not belong.
I cannot find myself.

I am sorry for all these things,
but you out of all people
must understand.

I cannot give in to you.
I cannot let you in the space.
In all my lonely spaces.
They are not big enough for two.

I am sorry you cannot call it home.
I cannot even say that for myself.

So how in the hell do you expect
to love me?
When I can barely love myself.

I am not who you think I am.

I am sorry.

Little Note:37

Thank you lover
for showing me how bad
things can get.

Because of you,
nothing worries me.

All else is nothing.

The mind makes everything
for what it really is.

Little Note:38

Your eyes and ears
will change.

Your mind and your heart
will change.

The air and the land
will change.

It all changes.

If it is not changing,
then it is all dead.

Change is everything.
Embrace it,
it is the only distraction
worth paying attention to.

If we.

Decisions In The Morning

If we move
too fast,
we will break
things.

If we move
too slow,
we will miss
things.

And if we do not move
at all,
we will not
see things for how
beautiful
they
truly are.

Choose wisely,
and if possible
blindly.

Maybe tomorrow.

Candles And Matches

Maybe tomorrow
that good-bye
will lead
to a new hello,
and maybe
this time you
will fuel
the fire in her
heart and
make her stay.

Fight for the people you love.

So good-byes will not end
in the burning sunset.

So the hellos
do not reoccur,
and the fire will
light the path to all
the lost people who are
caught in its flame.

We are magic.

Walking Into The Depths

We are magic.
We are moments.
We are dreams
and we are memories.

We are everything.

And in the depths
we swim deeper to discover
that we are not born
whole,
so we cannot be broken.

We are born in twos,
and we are searching...

Searching for the other piece,
that other person

to guide us home.

Smile.

Look Around You

Life is hard.
Life is hell.
Life is love.
Life is pain.

All of these things
are everywhere, and
there is no denying it.

We are born to suffer
from horrible truths,

but listen
there is so much to
smile about,

so why waste
your time wiping
down all those
tears.

Little Note:39

The pain has let me
fully bloom into the joys of life.

The pain is what makes
this human experience special.

Damnit, and it is terrible.

It is a human thing.

Little Note:40

All you have to do is remember.

Remember to make someone feel understood,

remember to make someone feel accepted,

and above all,

remember to make someone feel real.

Too much.

All Of You + Me

There is
too much noise
in me,
and too often
I feel
interrupted.

I need order.
I need love.
I need all of you
to calm the waves.

All of you to
set me free,

and

all of you
for all of me.

Save us.

Skulls Carry Bodies

Now they have taken
it all away from us.

Choices,
freedom, and
everything in between.

How do they expect us
to survive.

This world is mad,
it is a wasteland filled
with skulls.

It is all dying. It is all dead.

They shape us,
but only we can save us.

Separate. Separate. Separate.

You are sick. We all are.

We must question everything
that makes us who we
think we are.

Too much.

Too Much In Her

There is too much
fuel in her.
The world ignites her
fire, and
she works both ways.

She always has...

When she loves,
she loves too much,
and when she hates,
she hates too much.

And in between there is
so much wage,
so much that she loses
herself in the
moments.

And the closer she gets,
the further apart she wants
to be.

She just cannot get it together.

She is a reflection of all
the people she wants to love.

Hate is heavy.

Little Flame

I need you
to understand
that hate is heavy
so let it go.

No...

Burn it down,
burn it all fucking down,
and leave the regret
beneath the ash.

So when the fire
in your heart sparks,
everything you do
will burn too bright,
and too hot.

You will not dissolve into the night.

And the world
will never cease
to ignore the stars in you.

The world
will find peace
in your flame.

Brokenness.

Last Message

This is not a love poem.

This is me telling you how it is.

Bind me, my brokenness—
there is too much separation in me.

Leave my scars,
but devour all of the pain.

Kill my darling memories,
kill them all.

I want to love you.
I want to swallow
the sun and shine with someone like you.

Bind me, my body. My soul. My heart.
Construct me inside you.
Inside your body. Your soul. Your heart.

I love you. I love you. I love...
but this is not a love poem.

This is all the things
I need you to know before it is
too late.

Leave your heart little.

She Did Not Need Me

She left her heart little.
She left her heart childish.

And for her,
every little moment felt
like butterflies.

She did not want to believe
there was an end to love.

So she drowned in the seconds
beneath
the moment where magic
and stillness collide.

And every time she looked
into her very own eyes...

She was reminded
of how it felt
to be alive.

To Charise:

May your flame live
within me,
and continue to
inspire me
through every
waking hour.

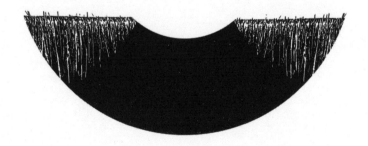

With open eyes I see the world,
with an open heart I see the souls,
and with an open mind I see it all differently.

Thank you for your time.

Robert M. Drake

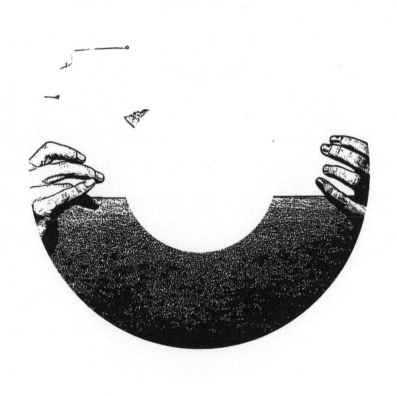

CHASING THE GLOOM

COMING SOON

SUN

ROBERT M. DRAKE

A NOVELLA
COMING SOON...

FLOWER

Also Available
ROBERT M. DRAKE
SPACESHIP

Also Available

ROBERT M. DRAKE
SCIENCE

BLACK
BUTTERFLY

Follow R. M. Drake
for excerpts and updates.

Facebook.com/rmdrk
Twitter.com/rmdrk
Instagram.com/rmdrk
rmdrk.tumblr.com